Zena Everett's

CRAZY BUSY

HOW TO GET MORE DONE IN A DAY THAN YOU DO NOW IN A WEEK

Simple ways to get your life back

Zena Everett's

CRAZY BUSY

HOW TO GET MORE DONE IN A DAY
THAN YOU DO NOW IN A WEEK.

Simple ways to get your life back

You need this book if:

- Your in-box controls your life

- You are always rushing

- At the end of the day you often feel disappointed that you didn't get any real work done

- You spend too much time in internal meetings You're too tired to exercise

- Sometimes you procrastinate

- You never have any time for you

  This book isn't about time management; it is about what you do with the rest of your life.

  This book will help you to stop repeating the patterns that keep you right where you are, and move you on to where you want to go.

Published by Filament Publishing Ltd
16, Croydon Road, Beddington
Croydon, Surrey CR0 4PA
www.filamentpublishing.com
+44 020 8688 2598

Printed by IngramSpark.

Please note that throughout the book where the last name
has not been provided, the name and some details have
most likely been changed.

Contents

Overview 6

Typical habits of a Crazy Busy person 7

How close to boiling point are you? 8

Start with the future you want to create 13

Where does your time go now? 14

Important/Urgent matrix 15

Blocker One: Fuzzy Focus 18

Blocker Two: Other People 21

Managing your emails 21

Shortening meetings 25

Preventing interruptions 28

Blocker Three: Procrastination 33

Design a routine and stick to it 35

Watch your perfectionist tendencies 37

Unwind & Unstuff: more cures for crazy busyness 39

Learn your limits and unwind 39

Unstuff your to-do list 40

There are only 24 hours in a day 42

Find a distraction 43

What does crazy busyness protect you from? 45

Crazy Busy - some speedy tips 47

References 49

About the author and contact details 51

Overview

I'm an Executive Coach, helping my clients to find and do great work.

My role is to help them change how they see themselves and the world. Coaching removes the obstacles they put in their way to success. It is powerful stuff, but it's not enough.

I've realised that there usually remains one last, big, blocker to them creating the life they want.

It's how they spend their most precious asset: their time.

They think that their work makes them stressed but that this is just how professional life is these days.

However, often the cause of their stress isn't their work at all.

It's how they work.

I've written this to share with you the ways that people have changed their working habits in order to manage their time far more effectively.

You don't need me to tell you the difference that would make to all aspects of your life.

Zena Everett

Typical work habits of a Crazy Busy person:

Work is a big part of our identity but it's just not working for us anymore. Digitisation has layered another layer of work on top of the real work. Consequently, we spend too much time chasing our tails in ever decreasing circles.

We finish work at the end of every day feeling that we have been crazy busy, but frustrated that we haven't actually got anything meaningful done. We are anxious about our job performance and security.

We feel out of control, unfulfilled and have lost our sense of professional pride and achievement.

We have 24 hours in a day, but it seems like everyone else must have more hours than we do, because we just don't get enough done.

I've put together thoughts and strategies from hundreds of people I've spoken to about this, to give you tactics to get your life back.

How close to boiling point are you?
How many of these crazy busy behaviours apply to you?

☐ When you get to work, the first thing you do is check your email. You deal with what's in your inbox, for as long as it takes. So far so good.

☐ You know the tasks you need to accomplish, but often don't start these until well after lunch, once you have had meetings and sorted out all urgent requests for attention/action from clients, colleagues, managers or people that work for you.

☐ Internal meetings over-run and often waste time on small talk. Senior people make pointless contributions that delay them further. Not everyone has completed their actions or read the papers, but they seem to get away with it. You're tempted to check your emails/ messages during meetings and if they are online meetings you have your eye on another screen too.

☐ You often eat lunch at your desk, in front of a screen. Probably similar food to the day before, because you can't be bothered to think about something different.

☐ By the time you start the tasks you intended to get on with, you are beginning to feel tired and less mentally sharp.

8

☐ Despite your workload, you are prone to procrastination and dithering.

☐ You are interrupted several times an hour, by emails and in person. Once you have dealt with their problem you find it hard to resume the task you were on.

☐ You like to please people and you find it hard to say no.

☐ Despite this, you can be sarcastic, snappy or passive-aggressive when people interrupt you.

☐ Working in an open plan office adds to your stress levels because you can't hide away to get your work done.

☐ You feel guilty for not spending more time with your team and direct reports. You dislike them even more for making you feel guilty. Why do they keep coming to you with stupid questions?

☐ You check social media when you take a quick break. This rarely makes you feel good. It takes a while to get going again when you get back on your work screen, so checking your emails again is an easy option.

☐ You start your 'real' work when the office is quieter, as other people start to leave.

☐ Having started some deep work, you find that you can't complete the task because other people haven't supplied all the information you need.

☐ You go home late, feeling resentful.

☐ You are out of the habit of playing with your children or talking to your partner. Sometimes you stay at work or go for a drink after work to avoid getting back before your kids go to bed.

☐ You get home, eat late, and watch TV to unwind, checking your phone periodically. You go to bed the wrong side of 11pm and you check messages and social media again in bed.

☐ You have a fragmented sleep before your early alarm call and might even check your phone when you wake up in the night.

☐ The first thing you do in the morning is check your phone again.

☐ You get cranky if you delay your morning caffeine fix. You lose patience with colleagues and the various idiots you encounter during the day.

☐ Your to-do-list gets longer/redder and you haven't time to update it, so it is spread over several pages of your notebook or whichever system you use.

☐ You have to work at weekends to actually get anything done.

☐ You constantly feel unproductive and ineffective.

☐ You don't want to put your hand up for promotion, as it feels safer to stay below the radar where people won't scrutinise your performance.

☐ You take your phone to the toilet – and check it when you are in there. You don't want extra responsibilities because that would make your work/life balance even worse.

☐ Your job description is out of date and you rarely get feedback from your manager. You are not 100% certain what your role is measured on, so you aren't really sure whether you are doing a good enough job or not.

☐ You have money to spend but not enough time to shop. You buy online regularly, daily even, but only get fleeting satisfaction from your purchases.

☐ Your work hours mean that you don't see your friends as often as you would like and you feel isolated and sometimes lonely.

☐ You feel too tired to exercise. You can't ignore your own well-being for much longer.

There are thirty statements here, some quite subjective. It's up to you how much Crazy Busyness you can tolerate, but I'd say anything over fifteen means that you are neglecting your longer time priorities and well-being. The closer you are to thirty, the closer you are to burn out.

Only you know the personal consequences of continuing like this.

Let's free you from this Crazy Busyness, so you can take back your time and regain a life: relationships, well-being and sense of purpose.

The starting point is identifying where you should be spending your time.

Start with the future you want to create

Identify five main areas of focus for your life, ideally three professional and two personal. This clarifies where you want to go.

What is most important to you? What will you deeply regret not spending time on, or achieving? (This is a more cheerful way of doing that life-coaching exercise of writing your obituary. Try that one too, if it helps you to realise what you are missing out on).

In the end column write the amount of time you spend on each priority, being honest with yourself. Total this column.

Priorities	% Time
1	
2	
3	
4	
5	
	Total time spent on your priorities

Abridged from: Peter Bregman's 18 Minutes to find your focus, master distractions & get the right things done

Where does your time go now?

If you aren't spending time on your own priorities, then you must be spending time on someone else's

There are dozens of theories for managing your time effectively - from eating elephants bite by bite, to boiling frogs slowly. We do the courses and read the books, but don't follow the theories because we haven't got time to manage our time! Real life gets in the way of great intentions.

What's 'real life'? Other people who interrupt you and demand your attention. They don't have to stand in front of you; they can distract you online, through email and social media.

I want to show you that you have a choice over how you spend your time and who or what you say no to.

Where does your time go now?

Reality Check

If you need some persuasion to work out where your time goes, then there is no better place to start than Stephen Covey's Time Management Matrix. Developed over 28 years ago, it is still the most logical way of understanding the discrepancy between how we want to spend our time and how we actually spend it. Covey's matrix evaluates tasks on two criteria: urgency and importance. Urgent tasks require immediate attention. Important tasks contribute to your values, priorities and long-term goals.

Q1 Important and Urgent	Q2 Important, Not Urgent
Q3 Urgent, Not Important	Q4 Not Important, Not Urgent

This is the kind of matrix people come up with on my Crazy Busy workshops. Try it for yourself, recording what you do over a week or whatever time-frame most accurately reflects your workload:

Q1 Important and Urgent	Q2 Important, Not Urgent
Meeting today's deadlines Fire-fighting Travel Crises	Your priorities Business planning Relationship developing New business Team development Organisational development Career conversations Networking strategy Deep, flow working Exercise, taking care of your health
Q3 Urgent, Not Important	Q4 Not Important, Not Urgent
Interruptions Answering any queries they could figure out themselves Some emails Some internal meetings Perfecting a task when good enough would do Internet surfing, hopping from one link to another Preparing too-long PowerPoint presentations	Procrastination & dithering Finessing work that is good enough Time-wasting people Networking meetings when a call would do Tasks below your pay scale that you should delegate 'Fixing to get ready' - over-preparing before you start a task Micro-managing and molly-coddling junior staff

Stephen R Covey, The 7 Habits of Highly Effective People

Most people spend too long in Q3, cranking the wheel to maintain the status-quo, having inefficient meetings, managing our inbox and disappearing down the rabbit hole of the internet.

We spend most of our day trying to get back to a neutral position, with a tidy in-box and nothing screaming out in front of us. When/if we get there we will feel in control and can move forward with the real work of Q2 – our priorities.

Q2 is the critical quadrant where we allocate time and energies to our own priorities, which will get us our long-term goals. Our goals and priorities, that is: not other people's goals and priorities. We need to get in Q2 as quickly as we can each day and spend as much time in it as possible.

Getting the right stuff done more quickly makes us more successful and gives us more leisure time.

What's really stopping us from taking back our time?

Here are three blockers why we faff around in Q3, instead of getting on with the real work of Q2.

Fuzzy focus. We don't know what our priorities are or where we should focus. We are confusing being busy with being effective but aren't sure what we should do with our time instead.

Other people. We know what we should be doing, but don't know how to manage the people that interrupt us. We need help in managing our emails, facilitating meetings, and saying an assertive, polite 'no'.

Procrastination. We have focus and techniques for dealing with people, but still delay getting on with what we have to do. Our own minds get in our way and stop us cracking on with what's important.

Let's fix each one, for good.

Blocker one: fuzzy focus

How can you manage your time effectively if you don't know your most important tasks?

This is the starting point for any personal effectiveness or on- boarding coaching when people start a new role. Where should you focus your time and energy? Specifically:

1. How do you know you are doing a good job?
2. What are the expectations you have to meet?
3. What are the key results areas of your job description?
4. Out of everything you do, what will you be measured on?
5. How does your work contribute to your manager's/ stakeholders'/clients' priorities?
6. What's the best use of your time?
7. How would other people describe your job function?

This seems obvious, but you'd be surprised how many people don't actually know the priorities of their role, particularly when they become more senior.

It can happen when they have been in an organisation a long time, taking on additional responsibilities as they go so their original job description becomes obsolete.

Or they work in a smaller business and have taken on other job functions in addition to their own, adding finance and HR to marketing and office management for example.

When I was a recruiter, we used to say that everything comes back to a job description – if you understand that, you'll make a successful hire. Once everyone is clear on the outcomes/deliverables required by the post-holder, so they can fully commit to achieving them.

If you don't know what outcomes you are supposed to achieve, then how can you focus your time and attention effectively?

Schedule a conversation to remove ambiguity.

Have a conversation with whoever pays your salary and has the most input into your career progression/goal achievement. 'I'm spinning so many plates at the moment, what's most important to the business?' Drop the things you do that aren't on the list, or get someone else to do them for you. You could be doing them a favour! They might enjoy them/learn from them/earn more money by doing them.

Rushing around being stupidly busy is not career enhancing. If you look as if you are at breaking point, you won't be given extra responsibilities that will enable you to take a step up. Your manager will worry that the extra burden will break you.

Successful people have a laser focus on getting important things done. They appear calm and in control, not frazzled. They aren't rushing to get small stuff done and everything on a long, to-do list. Look and behave like someone in the role above you, not like a stressed-out crazy person in the role you have now.

Slow down. Focus.

As Tim Ferriss, author of my favourite self-help book, The Four Hour Work Week, (all books mentioned are in the reference list on page 34), says: 'doing something unimportant well does not make it important'. Find out what 'important' is. People don't get fired for doing important work. People do get fired for being busy doing unimportant stuff. Get someone else to do your other routine tasks, or just stop doing them and see what happens. Be brave; take control of your own schedule.

What's the difference between good and outstanding performance in your role? That's where you should focus your time and energy. Don't wait to be given extra responsibility, take it. Now you are clear on what you should focus on, let's look at the next blocker: lack of technique for taking back your time from the people that hijack it.

Blocker two: other people

A crucial workplace skill is to stop other people hijacking our time with unnecessary emails, pointless meetings and interruptions.

This is Covey's Q3 – other people's urgent and not important to you. It's where the morning disappears as we trying to get back to square one, without interruptions and disturbances, so we can get on with the real work we planned to do.

People block us in three ways: emails, meetings and interruptions. Here's how to cut them off.

1.   Managing your emails

Manage your emails: don't let them manage you. Emails don't send themselves; people send them. You have to be proactive and train these people into how you are going to respond to and initiate emails. Should it really be our main form of communication?

Work an in-tray

Imagine you have an old-fashioned in-tray that dictates your workload. Check your inbox first thing for anything you need to know. Then switch off all email notifications and pop-ups for a couple of hours while you attack your priorities – a real or metaphorical in-tray. That means switching your phone off too. It's what people used to do before fast communication methods slowed productivity: they worked through their in-tray.

I know we try to be paperless now but I also know that people still print off their important emails. So use these prioritised documents to dictate the order of your work and start on them as close to first thing as you can.

Plan your priority tasks the night before so you can start them immediately.

Just do it! Stop staring at your screen.

Check in at lunchtime. You've got important stuff done, you feel energised and the sky hasn't fallen in because you weren't available.

Get back in the habit of talking.

Pick up the phone, walk across the office, and take the conversations back offline.

Email was never intended for conversations, debates (or to cover your proverbial). It's there to confirm or send lengthy documents quickly.

Want to build a trusted relationship? Call .

Sending information or confirmation? Email.

Make yourself a pleasant person to speak to and an easy person to get hold of. Trust me, you'll never be as overwhelmed by phone calls as you are by emails. Everyone else has got out of the habit of calling, with a subsequent loss in relationships and increased isolation. Talk to your colleagues, clients, managers and suppliers.

That's how you build trusted relationships.

Experiment with replacing emails with conversations. And notice how people feel comfortable in calling you back.

My clients have reported that booking in weekly 30 minute 1:1 meetings to catch up with team members can (counter-intuitively) saves them time, rather than responding to their endless email queries.

You are nipping problems in the bud and coaching them, encouraging them to think for themselves, rather than emailing you all the time.

Next time you are embroiled in an email dialogue, email back with 'call me' and take the relationship offline.

Lay out the ground rules.

What about your clients, customers, stakeholders? What if they send you an email and you don't jump on it? Won't they call your nearest competitor? I hear this all the time.

It's as if the clients can mind read that just for this two-hour period someone else takes priority over them.

If they are paying for this time, then that's fair enough. You jump really high. Otherwise, don't assume that they are expecting an instant response.

The client doesn't know if you are bathing your kids, running a marathon, or closing a huge prestigious deal for someone else. Reassure them by contracting clearly how you can work together.

It's OK to send a holding email to say that you've got their message and will respond in full by x time.

It's also OK to agree up front that all messages will be returned with 24 hours and all emails within 48 hours maximum. (Or whatever works).

It's OK to give them your personal phone number so they jump the queue in exceptional circumstances.

What's most important is how you treat them when you ARE available to them. Make them feel really special and wanted. In turn, they'll want more of you and your infectious enthusiasm to support them. That's how you become their trusted advisor. They want more of your time; so they are prepared to pay more for it.

Trying to please everyone in a fragmented way won't work long-term; it leads to burn-out. Better to have fewer clients who really value the relationship than trying to please loads of clients who don't. The model of being all things to everyone all the time is not sustainable.

Once you've managed your relationships, now attend to the practicalities of managing your inbox. I use Outlook and find having filters and rules helpful. Other people colour-code their messages according to the sender. Use any shortcuts and systems that work for you: it pays to invest some time in learning the short-cuts.

2. Shortening meetings

Ask anyone about how they spend their day and they complain about pointless, long, unplanned, badly facilitated, waffling, unstructured, distracted, ego-filled, hi-jacked and all round screamingly frustrating internal meetings. They even say they shouldn't have been in the meeting at all. External meetings on the main are ok, it's the internal meetings that seem to be the problem.

It is time for this boundary-less meeting culture to stop

I'm not going to detail what we all know already about tight agendas, starting on time, compulsory reading of papers and so on.

I'm just going to give you one simple tactic. My clients report back that it cuts their meeting time by about a third.

This is the question they ask that immediately anchors everyone into the objective of the meeting. It shames people out of hijacking it for their own agenda/ego.

What do we want to achieve in this meeting? Or a similar version: Can we get a consensus/agreement on what we want to achieve this morning?

Let's just remind ourselves of the purpose of this meeting.

You can ask this even if you aren't the chair or organiser. It puts the spotlight on why you are all together.

It's not rocket science, but it is magic. It's the goal. Identify the real, goal of the meeting and then the obvious solution often becomes clear more quickly.

Ask it at the beginning. Straight in, before the rest of the agenda and the usual fifteen minutes of small talk.

Notice the immediate difference in the participants – how people sit up and pay attention, drop their phones and look at you.

Either tell them what you want to achieve in the meeting or get their consensus, as appropriate. If this takes a while, fine. If people have different interpretations of what you are trying to achieve, better to get agreement at this stage or risk an entirely pointless meeting.

Follow it up with who should contribute what, and how long you need.

Give people the gift of time. 'We should be able to do that within 30 minutes,' will make you the most popular person in the building.

If what other people want to talk about doesn't contribute to the agreed purpose of the meeting, then they soon learn to keep quiet or risk looking foolish.

What difference would it make to you, and your organisational culture, if your meetings took one third less time? Try it. Pick a notoriously long internal meeting next week and ask this question right at the beginning:

'Let's take a step back and remind ourselves of what we want to achieve in this meeting?'

3. Preventing interruptions

You finally get down to getting some real work done. You've scheduled it, started it and are getting absorbed in it. You've switched off your emails and turned your phone off. It feels great to be concentrating on something significant.

You're in that state of optimum concentration and deep working called flow. You feel confident that your skills are up to the challenge. You are nicely in your comfort zone, losing yourself in the important task in front of you.

Can you remember when you last worked in a flow state? If I ask this question to a room of people, generally at least ten percent will have no memory of it at all.

McKinsey research says that working in flow means we are five times more productive than our steady state colleagues. If you spend Monday in flow, you'll do the equivalent of their whole week.

You've got there. So far, so good.

Then along comes one of your team, oblivious to your blissful state of textbook flow working: 'Hey, have you got a minute, I just want to run something past you?'

Peter Bregman quotes a study conducted by Microsoft Corporation on interruptions. They taped twenty-nine hours of people working and found that on average they were interrupted four times per hour. (That seems quite low, compared to many of the people I talk to about this).

Here's the important bit:

Forty percent of the time people did not resume the task they were working on before they were interrupted.

And, worse:

The more complex the task, the less likely the person was to return to it.

They don't return to their deep work; they never get back in flow. They pick up something easier. 'Easier' usually means less significant.

Let's be clear. This is not multi-tasking. This is just switch-tasking from one task to another and kidding ourselves we are productive.

How do you stop interruptions?

You can lock your office door, if you have one, and who has an office to themselves these days? You can work at home, or in a meeting room, or hide in a coffee shop.

Most clients tell me they have to resort to these tactics to get anything done, but it is unrealistic to try and shut the world out every time you need to do some deep work. Most of us like to please others and find it hard to say 'not now' when someone is standing in front of you. Perhaps we just don't have the vocabulary to say 'go away' politely.

Either way, it's often easier just to deal with the problem then try to explain that now's not a good time.

Let's try and stop them getting in front of you: stopping the interruption before it happens.

It comes down to boundaries: ring-fencing your time when you can be interrupted and protecting the time when you can't be.

Schedule time when you can be interrupted

Avi was a director of a small consulting business. His priority was to generate new business for the firm, as well as managing a team and informally mentoring others.

New business wasn't coming in because he spent his entire week fire-fighting, dealing with existing clients and hand-holding his team. He liked to be needed, so it flattered his ego that people wouldn't make decisions without him. He was hard to get hold of because he was always rushing from one demand to another. Consequently, he was preventing other people from making progress on their projects because they needed to talk to him.

His role was measured on new business revenue. He complained he couldn't do this because his team interrupted him so much, he had no time to pick up the phone. He was frustrated, his team was frustrated, his CEO was highly frustrated.

He did two things:

He made himself available after 4 pm every single day, so people knew they could come with queries then and he'd have time to listen to them. He forced himself to shut his screen, turn his chair around, fix a smile, and give them undivided attention.

It wasn't always easy for him to be present in the office and available every day, but he managed to make it happen with very few exceptions and, most importantly, to stick to the new routine. It's no good doing this for a few days then slinking back to your old habits: that's going to destroy trust.

Avi also booked short but frequent 1:1 meetings with his team, often twenty-minute catch ups, with no time-wasting preamble, in between more formal meetings. He knew what everyone was doing and they were all on the right track. They had airtime with him and he was able to identify potential issues before they escalated.

The results were obvious and immediate.

By scheduling more time with his team, he had more time without them. By and large, they learnt to leave him alone because they had the reassurance of knowing when he would be available to them. He could get on with his priorities during the rest of the day and meet his own targets.

Decent communication enabled him to become a better manager. With his guidance and encouragement, his team learnt to think for themselves, improved their skills and relied on him less. In time, he was able to cut back on some of the 1:1s because they weren't so necessary. They loved him for giving them whole-hearted attention and his appraisal rating for leadership improved.

Prevent most unwanted interruptions by scheduling time when you are available and can be interrupted.

I've seen this work with entire teams and departments. They schedule times during the day/week/month when they are available and happy to help etc. They expected the announcement to cause friction and were invariably surprised and almost disappointed that it went unnoticed.

On the contrary, showing the world how efficient you are at managing your time can only be a positive.

Blocker three: procrastination

You've got a tool-kit now for managing your mail, switching off your phone and preventing interruptions. You're judicious about social media use. But you're still not getting on with the task.

What's stopping you?

In a beautiful irony, before starting this section I've replied to some emails, edited a seminar proposal that was already fine, arranged to see a friend, sent some LinkedIn invitations, bought a present online, drank two cups of tea and paid a bill before it was due.

It felt great. But who am I kidding?

Doing something unimportant well does not make it important.

I was being efficient with my time, but not effective. It's like colouring in your revision diary. You're busy, but you aren't revising.

Scott Smith, a US motivational coach, brilliantly calls procrastination 'fixing to get ready': getting ready to get ready to do stuff.

Why do we faff about, distract ourselves and delay starting the tasks we intended to get on with?

I don't think it's anything to do with liking or not liking what we have to do. I am very focused, treasure my writing time and had every intention of doing this today.

Schedule time and location

One theory is that I had too much time to do the task. I had four hours spare at home, which is a rare treat, but I hadn't made a plan for how to use it effectively. I started with easy wins, that I could squeeze in anytime between more important tasks.

Like many people, I am most productive when I schedule a time to do something and then go to a location specifically to do it. I start it straight away. Time is limited (you can only string out so many cups of coffee in a cafe, or book a room for a finite period).

My brain doesn't stray onto distractions because I don't associate that place with other more fragmented tasks - the routine administration I do in my home office for example.

Many people have said that they get more done when travelling than they do in the office, both because of eliminating interruptions but also because they planned to do something specific in that time and place. I wrote most of my first book, Mind Flip, in hotels and on trains.

The golden rule of all time management is: if it's not scheduled, it doesn't get done.

Ideally, schedule a time and a place to do your most significant tasks. We block out meetings in our diaries, so why not block out time for tasks too?

Design a routine and stick to it

Newly self-employed, and people who work from home sometimes, like me, seem to be particularly prone to procrastination.

We'll 'just' unload the dishwasher, put in some washing, check the headlines, etc., before we start. How we spend our day can depend on our mood and what we feel ready to take on. We have a slow build up to getting ready, regardless of our intentions.

An 'impromptu' anything can easily distract us from our priorities.

We're all guilty of this, but I've learnt the hard way that the financial and creative freedom of working for myself doesn't mean a freedom from professional norms or – that word again – boundaries.

On the contrary, we need to be a tough boss. We need more discipline then we might have in an open plan office where working or appearing to work, is the norm.

We have to surround ourselves with structure, in order to be creative within that structure.

Executive Coach Steve Chandler talks great common sense about the beauty of a routine.

Forget about working on your mindset or attitude to get something done. He says that you just need a routine, irrespective of your frame of mind – what he calls 'a committed amount of time to devote to something, no matter what.'

You don't have to wait until you feel like doing something.

Most schools make the children do their maths lesson when it is timetabled, not when they feel like it. We need the same professionalism as a six-year-old. (Please don't email me if your kids are educated with a relaxed timetable, I realise there are wonderful exceptions to every rule).

Just do it. Same time, every day, every week. If that doesn't work for you, then change the routine.

No procrastination, just stick to the routine, chunking up your diary into ninety-minute ish periods of timetabled tasks.

All you have to do is ... START.

Watch your perfectionist tendencies

Worrying about being perfect not only stops you from being perfect, it leads to procrastination and inertia.

Do you like to do everything at the last minute, right up to the deadline?

You've got an important report to write, due in by Friday morning. If you block out time early in the week to write and edit it, you stand a fair chance of producing a decent quality document. If you do it over Thursday night and the early hours of Friday morning, you are giving yourself a get-out clause for a sub-standard result, 'If I only had more time, it would have been perfect.'

You are protecting yourself from the fear of failure. If you'd wholeheartedly thrown yourself into writing the report, and it still wasn't up to your uncompromisingly high standards, you'd have to deal with that. This way, your perfectionist tendencies have held you back, protecting you from facing up to your perceived sub-standard performance and failures.

Rather than giving you a safety net, this avoidance behaviour creates even more stress and anxiety. Your delaying and last minute approach likely creates stress for the people you work with too.

Our parents' work ethic inspired many of us to get a good education and achieve in our own careers. But we can take this too far.

Perfectionists are created when they are criticised as children for less than perfect performance: the one spelling they got wrong, not the nineteen they got right. 'If a job's worth doing it's worth doing well' was the mantra at home. They adopt this philosophy in order to please and sometimes survive.

Life is just too full now to do everything perfectly. Some jobs need to be perfect; some just need to get done.

Manage your reluctance to start, and finish, tasks by sticking to your routine and scheduled tasks and location.

Reduce the pressure you put on yourself and know when good enough is absolutely fine.

What you do is significantly more important than how you do it.

Unwind & unstuff: more cures for crazy busyness

Crazy busyness does your career no favours. Chill out, restore your energy and negotiate your workload. Find distractions. Look like you can cope with more responsibilities, not that you are about to crack up.

We're aiming to do more deep, flow working, and far less shallow, switch tasking. Deep working drains you of energy so you need to take proper breaks in between.

Learn your limits and unwind

Your productivity will be boosted if you spend more time unwinding, rather than staring at your screen.

Author and Professor Cal Newport quotes research conducted by Ernst and Young on its workers in 2006, showing that for every extra ten hours spent on vacation, yearly performance reviews went up by eight per cent.

Look around you – do people doing better than you seem to make a greater contribution in less hours? I'd place a bet that they don't work as many hours as you do. They get more important work done in less time and take more time to unwind. This restores their energy so that the standard of their work becomes even higher.

Successful people stick to the work that has the greatest impact. They are smart about where they focus their resources: higher value, lower hanging. They delegate or just drop tasks that don't contribute to their objectives. In between, they unwind and enjoy life. They are effective, successful and interesting. Their energy is infectious: clients and staff want to work with them.

The people who regularly stay late and don't take their holidays are the ones who make the most errors. They are tired, snappy, put- upon. It does them no favours.

Promotion doesn't depend on presenteeism anymore. Some judicious hanging around the office after hours might help your prospects, but doing visibly great work and using your charm will get you much further, even if you are an intern.

Look like you are working hard but still have the capability to take on more responsibility; not that you are already on your knees!

Un-stuff your to-do list

It's stressful and depressing finishing work every day with only a fraction of your to-do list done. It just turns into a neat list of reasons to feel guilty and rubbish about yourself.

Make sure your expectations are realistic and don't try to do too much.

So many books been written about to-do lists. We'd read them all if we had more time and probably be even more overwhelmed.

The advice that has worked best for me (from Tim Ferriss) was to get rid of my to-do list altogether. Hurray.

I've now got a list of my goals/priorities/objectives/projects and then a list of sub-tasks that contribute to each one. My random, stuffed, to- do list, is now several lists of sub-tasks under each priority heading.

I feel much more in control.

Every day I scribble a check-list of things I have to do from that sub- task list and also from my daily schedule. Inevitably there are also reminders of minor things I need to do to keep the show on the road at home and work.

I keep it realistic: challenging enough to keep me motivated, but not so much to do that it tips me into anxiety. I don't want to waste time on worrying about what I have to do, I just want to crack on with it.

It doesn't matter how you manage your to-do list, as long as you have a system that enables you to be effective. I like handwritten daily task lists, not least because it's more satisfying scribbling them off. If I keep shifting tasks from one day to the next I either do them, schedule them in my diary to do them, pay someone to do them for me, make a calendar note to remind me of them at a more appropriate time or eliminate them altogether.

Always on that list is one 'big' action each day. This is to move my business forward; perhaps a call to build a relationship or get new work, build a partnership etc.

I know lots of people advise aiming for three of these, but just one works for me. When I aimed for three, but only got one done, my mood used to sink and I felt like I'd failed that day. Invariably now I do my first call, feel positive, and sneak in some more.

Like all career management tactics, this is all about small, daily incremental actions, not great intentions you can't keep up with.

There are only 24 hours in a day

I've had startling conversations with frazzled people who had taken on more than they are physically capable of doing.

One had taken on an extra project, forgetting to first agree which parts of their existing workload they could pass on to someone else. Whilst you need to show that you have capacity to take on more responsibility, clearly that doesn't mean you are going to eat into your weekends to get it done.

An Audit Senior I coached returned to work after maternity leave on a three-day week, but her billable hours target was the same as when she was full-time. She was so grateful for a part-time opportunity that she hadn't pointed out the obvious maths. Her company weren't bothered: they saved on her bonus and knew she'd work when she was at home because she was so 'conscientious'. Conscientious? Crazy.

This is a guaranteed path for failure. We're humans, not machines.

The workplace is no respector of martyrs – assertiveness and negotiation skills are far more highly valued then a boundless capacity for being a doormat. Is it time you had a conversation about what is realistic for you to achieve?
What's your highest and best use- where can you make the greatest contribution in the time available to you? Stick to that and you won't go far wrong.

Find a distraction

Tasks expand to fit the time available. Taking away time sounds counterintuitive, but I've found that a challenging distraction, rather than adding to the craziness, makes people happier and much more effective with their remaining time.

Katharine was the UK Head of a global business. Married with a young family, she had a fantastic, all-consuming role. She'd grown up in the business and couldn't quite believe how far she'd come.

Her imposter syndrome manifested itself in her spending too much time in the weeds - she just couldn't let go. She micromanaged her very capable team and knew too much about the detail of the business, neglecting the strategy that was her primary role responsibility.

She worked extremely long hours, doing her own work and meddling in other people's too – even going into work at weekends to help junior staff in events they were running. Rolling up your sleeves occasionally is helpful, but she neglected to lead the business and lost capable managers who felt they weren't growing under her leadership.

How did she fix the problem? She returned to her old childhood love of competitive dressage; an expensive, time-consuming passion.

This was a huge distraction. If she wasn't riding, she was with her family, or at work.

At work, she only had time available to stick to her role function. She set her strategy, ensured she had a capable and motivated team in place, and didn't have time to micro-manage or mollycoddle. Having a passion outside work and home replenished her energy and focus in all areas. I'm sure it wasn't easy to spin the plates, but the self-esteem boost she got from dressage boosted her confidence at work too.

What does Crazy Busyness protect you from?

Why do many of us fall into this trap of crazy busyness? Humans are happier when we are busy. It makes us feel useful, needed, relevant. 'I'm so busy' has become a badge of honour. It doesn't make us better at our jobs and has horrible consequences for our health, happiness and relationships.

Here's Social Scientist Brene Brown's take on it:

'Crazy-busy' is a great amour, it's a great way for numbing. What a lot of us do is that we stay so busy, and so out in front of our life, that the truth of how we're feeling and what we really need can't catch up with us.'

I'm not suggesting being less busy - just being busy on the right things and gaining more control of your time.

Switching off, then switching on whole-heartedly.

Doing one thing at once. Sticking to your own job, not being busy micromanaging other people's work, or doing their work for them because that way it'll be done right.

Having the time to look at people when they speak in meetings.

Taking time to think, focus, be creative, find solutions and do your best work.

Don't sleepwalk into unhealthy, unproductive and damaging habits by not taking stock of how you spend your time.

Take the time to fall back in love with what you do and find the meaning in your work, not in the busyness of it.

Crazy Busy - some speedy tips

- Fuzzy focus makes us confuse being crazy busy with being effective. What are your priorities and where should you focus your time and energy?

- If you aren't crystal clear on what outstanding performance in your role looks like, then schedule a conversation to remove ambiguity.

- Don't waste precious time on unimportant tasks. What can you cut back on, speed up, delegate or stop doing?

- Slow down. Look and behave like you are ready for promotion, not like a frazzled crazy busy person.

- Manage your emails; don't let them manage you. Want to build a trusted relationship? Call, don't email.

- Give the gift of time by running shorter meetings. Start by asking 'what do we want to achieve in this meeting?' to focus everyone on the purpose and find a faster solution.

- Block out times and location to do your deep, flow working and eliminate interruptions.

- Schedule more short 1:1 meetings and informal catch-ups. By spending more time with your team, you'll get more time without them to get on with your own work.

- Design a routine and stick to it. Don't wait until you are in the mood to start something. Just start it. Your mood will catch up. Good enough is usually fine; tasks rarely need to be perfect.

References

Peter Bregman (2011), *18 Minutes to find your focus, master distractions & get the right things done*, Orion Books Ltd.

Brene Brown (2012), *Daring Greatly: How the Courage to be Vulnerable Transforms the Way we Live, Love, Parent and Lead*, Avery Publishing Group.

Steve Chandler & Rich Litvin (2013), *The Prosperous Coach: Increase Income & Impact for You and Your Clients*, Maurice Bassett

Mihaly Csikszentmihalyi (2008), *Flow: The Psychology of Optimal Experience*

Stephen R Covey (first published 1988), *7 Habits of Highly Effective People*, Free Press

Tim Ferriss (2007), *The 4-Hour Workweek: Escape 9-5, Live Anywhere, and Join the New Rich*, Crown Publishing Group.

McKinsey Quarterly (January 2013), *Increasing the Meaning Quotient at Work*

Michael Neenan & Windy Dryden (2002), *Life Coaching: A Cognitive-Behavioural Approach*, Routledge

Cal Newport, (2016), *Deep Work, Rules for Focused Success in a Distracted World*, Hachette Book Group

Scott Smith, www.MotivationToMove.com

I'd love to know what's been helpful to you in this book or any of your favourite strategies that I haven't included.

Please email me: zena@zenaeverett.com
Follow me: @zenaeverett1
Sign up to my mailing list: www.zenaeverett.com

About the Author

Zena Everett is an international executive coach and a speaker on workplace and personal productivity.

She has spent a lifetime helping people to find great work. When she followed up with them, they inevitably told her that they spent most of their time on Fake Work and very little time being effective, never mind great (and often they only managed that when everyone else had gone home).

Zena wrote her Crazy Busy™ sessions to help them get more done in a day than they do now in a week. More of the right work, that is.

For more information please visit www.zenaeverett.com or email her: zena@zenaeverett.com.

Here's a snapshot of Zena's Crazy Busy™ sessions for quick-bite training, conferences, away-days and offsites. Email zena@zenaeverett.com to discuss options.

1. Crazy Busy: How to get more done in a day than you do now in a week

Do you go home feeling frustrated that, despite working really hard, you still didn't get enough done? Do you sometimes feel overwhelmed? Are you always rushing? Going to bed wired and tired?

Crazy Busy ™ is an engaging, highly interactive session to explore how we actually spend our time now and the hijackers that block our personal productivity.

You will leave with tangible actions to put into immediate effect that will help you to:

- Work on your priority tasks, to get your real work done.

- Block out time to concentrate in 'flow' - a state of optimum performance proven to boost productivity.

- Manage the hijackers – meetings, emails and other people with conflicting priorities.

- Push back on unreasonable demands.

- Gain clarity on your priority tasks – your 'antelopes' and spend less time on low priority 'chipmunks'.

- Quit trying to multi-task and instead switch from one task to another more quickly.

- Gain the courage to block distractions so you can achieve tasks in half the time.

- Improve cross-team collaboration.

- Get the right things done and stop doing the wrong things.

2. A follow up session to this, about four weeks later:

Crazy Busy Follow-Up: Under the bonnet

A follow-up to the Crazy Busy ™ session to look in more detail at the hijackers that still inhibit your productivity. These often include:

- 'Corridor kidnappers' who interrupt you and divert you from your priorities.

- People who still won't provide agendas for meetings or run their meeting efficiently.

- Long email chains.

- Managers/colleagues who don't provide clear briefings so you end up repeating the work.

- Other people who live in Quadrant 3 - everything is Urgent but only Important to them.

- Your own perfectionism, procrastination or people-pleasing tendencies that stop you from pushing back or make you spend too much time on less significant tasks.

This session will explore any changes you have made so far and give you more practical solutions to getting the right work done.

3. A session for managers and above (which should be held after the first Crazy Busy session, to feed-back some observations of where you could me more effective)

Crazy Busy for Leaders: An extra day

Do you want your teams to be 20% more Productive? Collaborative? Successful? And work less hours?

What difference would it make to your business if:

- Your staff were FIVE times more productive?

- Collaboration and communication improved?

54

- They got more focused tasks done each day?

- They stopped the illusion of multi-tasking and instead completed tasks then moved quickly to the next one, eliminating down-time?

- Phones were switched off and people concentrated on their tasks?

- Meetings were planned and talked?

- They quit procrastinating and got on with the right tasks more effectively?

- They worked at the top of their comfort zones and were able to really think?

In Crazy Busy ™ we will explore ways to be five times more effective and the hijackers that can prevent this.

People get in their own way, whilst organisations create processes and rituals that create productivity-killing 'organisational drag'. These are proven to waste up to 20% of our time each week: that's a lost day.

You wouldn't waste any other resource like this, but we squander precious talent by not enabling them to get focused work done.

Great leaders set clear visions, objectives and performance standards. Then they set up the conditions for outstanding performance: environments where people do their best work, push themselves, use their heads and feel great about it. This is the aim of leadership and the goal of this session.

Team Offsite Option:
Crazy Busy and Bears

One of the objectives of Crazy Busy is to block out time for deep 'flow' working. Many of us have forgotten how to do this – and can't cope without our phones.

Here's a way to rewire your brains and take your team on an event they'll never forget.

We combine two bespoke training sessions exploring Crazy Busyness with two nights deeply absorbed watching Brown Bears in their natural habitat.

Full details, dates & cost: here: https://www.zenaeverett.com/crazy-busy-bears-team-training/

Also published by Zena Everett:

Mind Flip: Change the Way You Think About Yourself and
Reinvent Your Future (Second Edition)
ISBN: 978-1-912635-55-9

Mind Flipping: to flip your focus away from yourself and
instead look outwards – on to the value you add and the
problems you, uniquely, can solve for other people.
#itsnotaboutyou

Graham Norton believes that this philosophy will help you
transform the way you look at your career – forever!

Comprehensive, smart and accessible - an excellent guide to successful career management.

Alan Stewart, Partner, Blackwood Group

Mind Flip is the must-read career manual for anyone looking to change jobs, achieve promotion or find more fulfilling work.

It is when you are too busy to take a step back and focus on YOU that you really need to pick up this powerful book. Based on Zena's understanding of organisational psychology and cognitive behaviour disciplines coupled with her very real world experience, she has triumphed with a highly insightful and practical book that is a pleasure to read.

Louise Brett, Partner Deloitte Digital & Head of Consulting, Women in Leadership

Zena really challenges the status quo in Mind Flip. If you are fed up in your job, want a change or new direction; you need to take personal responsibility to do something about it. This book can help you. Zena talks through how to make shifts and developments to your career and think about what you can deliver to your boss to create a win-win outcome.

James Bennet MBE, Director, Ernst & Young LLP

Read Mind Flip to understand what you do best, sell yourself with confidence; and find the courage to ask for what you want.

David Goldstone, Director, Osprey Clarke, Executive Search

Zena's advice is brilliant. It's sensible as well as entertaining and it's based on years of real-life experience in recruitment.

Sir Richard John Evans, former President of Wolfson College, Cambridge and Provost of Gresham College

It's refreshing to see a career book that unpicks the bias in organisations – and in our own heads – that stops us from fulfilling our dreams. Whether you're facing the glass ceiling or the class ceiling, this book helps you understand how to break through it, and get on.

Mary Creagh MP

Available from Amazon (paperback and Kindle), to order from Foyles, Waterstones and your local bookshop, or from my website, www.zenaeverett.com

Printed in October 2021
by Rotomail Italia S.p.A., Vignate (MI) - Italy